Memories of Burma

David Olson

Inkling Press
Menlo Park, California

Copyright © 2011 by David Olson. All rights reserved. No part of this publication may be reproduced or utilized in any form or by any means, electronic or mechanical, including photocopying, recording, or by any information storage or retrieval system, without written permission from the publisher, except for the inclusion of quotations in a review. For further information, you may contact the publisher.

Published by:
Inkling Press
P.O. Box 2598
Menlo Park, CA 94026
www.inklingpress.com

Photographs by the author.

Cover design by David Olson and Audrey Landgraf. Initial editing by Lynn Rogers. Final editing/layout/formatting by Audrey Landgraf.

Printed and bound in the United States of America.

ISBN 9780982620328

Library of Congress Control Number 2011923370

First Printing, 2011

In memory of

Mack Ramlow
and
Helena Kirkham

Introduction

In 1956 my parents, older brother, younger sister, and I moved from Minneapolis, Minnesota to Rangoon, Burma. I was fourteen. The Burmese country, and especially the people, made a huge and long lasting impression on me. After my family and I moved back to the States in 1958 I never forgot my Burmese friends; the local kids and the kids from international families.

While en-route to Burma, our family stopped for a few days in Tokyo, Japan. We met a Christian missionary who was living there. He took us on a tour of the city and then to a fine dinner at a Geisha house and there, told us a story.

He said that once we arrived in Burma one of the first things we would notice was the smell. Especially the smell of the fish market because it was so overpowering and offensive. He went on to say that within a month or two, we would grow to love the aroma. This was, he said, a part of Asia.

He was right on all accounts. In Rangoon the smells were at once indeed overwhelming, but again, within a short period of time I had learned to love the experience. Not just the smell but also the activity bursting forth at the fish and other markets, the sight of the merchants selling their wares and, especially, the sounds. Everywhere there was music, the sounds of gongs, and *laughter plus the sing-song dialects of the people on the street.*

All of these memories continue to haunt me to this day. I almost feel lost without those thoughts and am relieved when I remember them.

Writing this story helps bring back those precious times and the wonderful people associated with those memories.

After some decades, my Burmese-related friends from the mid 1950's and I got together to catch up on our adult lives and remember fond times in Burma. We held reunions for many years. Several of us returned to Burma in 2005. I kept a diary of that trip, recording every special moment.

Having retired from my job in the airline industry in 2010, I started to write a memoir of my teenaged years in Burma. I had enrolled in a class titled "Creative Writing from the Right Brain," taught by Lynn Rogers, through MetroEd in San Jose, California. She helped me improve my writing skills and encouraged me to expand the tales of my memoirs.

I wanted to combine my 2005 diary with my earlier teenaged, memories of Burma. In my 2005 diary I scribbled references such as, " ... that reminds me of the time in 1956 when we kids . . . "

I needed to tie my early Burmese experiences to my current adult impressions of Burma. I started with the recent tour and then recalled people, events, and impressions as I remembered them from the mid 1950's when I was just a teenaged boy. That's what this book is about.

ACKNOWLEGEMENTS

Lynn Rogers was a great help, supplying ideas and encouragement. Fellow classmates in Lynn's writing class were supportive and eager to hear more details about my early life in Burma. I appreciate their interest and comments. Lynn Rogers and Audrey Landgraf were very helpful with regard to editing and final format.

Memories of Burma

2005 BURMA (MYANMAR) DIARY

– How I found my teenage years, and more, after 40 years –

By
David Olson
San Jose, CA

Personal note from Win Aung, friend of author David Olson:

David's late father, Myron Olson, worked with my late father Chelk Ping Lee, then Burma's Director of Technical Education under the Ministry of Education, establishing Myanmar's (then known as Burma) first-ever technical and vocational education system. Reading David's account of his re-visit to the country, his first in 40 years, brings back much fond remembrances of my own. Convinced that there are others who will enjoy David's interesting account of his personal journey, laid out in his inimitable prose, I have talked him into letting me post it on the Web so as to share it more widely. Thank you, David.

Win Aung
Potomac, MD
September 6, 2006

Chelk Ping Lee, Win Aung's father

Myron Olson, David Olson's father, and a technical instructor

Memories of Burma

Burma Revisited

How to begin? Actually this adventure began back in 1956. I was 14 years old, my brother Jerry was 16 and my sister Ginny was 10. My dad took a sabbatical from his teaching job at Dunwoody, a technical school in Minneapolis, to help set up a technical school in Rangoon, Burma through a grant from the Ford Foundation. Our entire family moved to Rangoon and lived there for a little more than two years. That whole experience is another story altogether. We moved back to the U.S. in midsummer of 1958.

Skipping ahead 40 years, I'm married, have two children and am living in San Jose, California. I worked for United Airlines as an A.M.T. (aircraft maintenance technician, i.e., mechanic). In early 1998 I got a phone call from Lauri Flach, one of the teenagers we were with in Rangoon. She, her sister Edie, Betsy Lindeman-Flint and another Rangoon brat (as we called ourselves), Diane, then Rydell now Hatheway, were trying to get a reunion together and called those for whom she had telephone numbers and addresses with hopes of reaching as many people as possible.

Memories of Burma

A long story staying long; Lauri, Edie, Betsy and Diane organized our first Rangoon reunion held at Algonquin Park near Washington D.C. It was such an overwhelming success that we began a series of reunions about one year apart with more people coming to each one:

Oct. 1998 Algonquin Washington D.C.
Oct. 2001 Boulder Creek, California
Oct. 2002 back to Algonquin
Oct. 2003 Myrtle Beach, South Carolina

At the 2003 reunion at Myrtle Beach arranged by Sally Anne and husband Harold, a special guest, Jai Kwong arrived from Hong Kong. It seems like each reunion someone special shows up. I say, "special" because it's that person's first reunion and we haven't seen them since 1958. Anyway, Jai suggested that we return to Rangoon for our next reunion. I'm sure others had the same reaction that I did at the time, that it was a pipe dream. It just didn't seem possible. Too far away, too much planning, too expensive.

I played with maybe going and with not going for most of the next year. I ended up going for multiple reasons:

Memories of Burma

- I turned 63 in Oct. of 2004 and if I didn't go then, I knew I never would.
- Going with a group of old friends was a definite advantage over going alone.
- Looking back, my life in Burma was so very important to me that I knew that if I didn't go, I'd be kicking myself forever.
- I had, and still have, dreams about my time in Burma; all good dreams, all good times.
- Finally, I loved that experience so much that I knew I had to relive it one more time.

Upon reflecting, it was somewhat selfish on my part because although they would have wanted to go, Jerry and Ginny couldn't go. The folks needed their care and Ginny was recovering from foot surgery and having difficulty walking. So I became the representative of the Olson clan. What follows is a day by day account of our trip that began Feb. 1 until my return on Feb. 14, 2005.

Feb.1, Tuesday

I was very nervous about going. Although I fly often, this was my first full fare flight and also my first "e-ticket" at that. It turned out to be a "piece of cake." All I needed was to hand the agent my passport and I was booked from San Francisco to Narita, Japan to Bangkok with assigned seats. I'd never really traveled like that before as usually I fly standby. It was nice not having to wait for my name to be called on the standby list. As it turned out, if I had gone standby I could have flown 1st class to Narita, but I never would have made a flight for the rest of the trip.

Feb. 2, Wednesday

It was about a seven hour flight to Japan, with a two hour layover and six hours to Bangkok. I arrived at 11:30PM on Feb. 2 since I passed over the International Date Line. I met Carolyn Bacon–Coughlin when she arrived and we shared a taxi to our respective hotels. Carolyn went to the Peninsula hotel where Oliver, Susan and Lauri were staying and I to the Sheraton Orchid Hotel where Edie, Bill, Diane and Allen were staying. I got to bed about 1:30AM-tired but wired.

Feb. 3, Thursday

Next morning, those of us at my hotel had breakfast together and then I got talked into going to a massage parlor with them. Quite an experience! There were five of us in one room getting worked over by what appeared to be teenage Thai girls. I'd been suffering from a damaged rotator cuff and this was not a good time to "feel the pain." That was my first and last massage – ever.

Had a Thai lunch and shared two taxis to the airport where we met Jai and flew on to Yangon, which was formerly known as Rangoon. Arrived at about 7:30PM. Jai had a tour guide named Franco who met us and handled our baggage and had cars waiting to escort us to his wife Winwin's house. He had an entire staff that carried bags, opened doors, tipped others when appropriate, drove us around, arranged meals, washed and pressed clothes, and served drinks. My God- this is a great way to live!

So we went to Winwin's house on Than Lwin road. This home is more of a mansion than a house. Winwin had room enough to sleep all 12 of us. We had a grand meal there, some drinks and then to bed. By the way, Joe and Caroline Stepanek were already there, as they had arrived the day before.

Feb. 4, Friday

Winwin, by the way, was one of the most delightful, beautiful ladies that I had set eyes on, with the exception of my wife Mary. The next morning was a breakfast buffet with eggs cooked to order. Also fruit, breads and juices. It was grand. Then one of the drivers took us all to look for our old homes. First stop was Kirkham's school. I have to say that Rangoon has changed so much that almost every thing is unrecognizable. Yes, it was the Kirkham's school, but it just didn't look right. For one thing, to get to the building we had to walk up a road that approached it from the back side. The building was on a hillside overlooking University Ave., but we always arrived by going directly to the front from University Ave. Also the front entrance wasn't right. Instead of a big door directly in front, we now entered by a side door. The place looked smaller than I remembered. Stepping back as far as we could, all of a sudden the mystery was solved. The house had been cut in half. Workers were in the process of renovating it. There was a fence between the two halves. When we visualized the buildings connected, yes! It was the old school.

At this point everyone's memories went into high gear. Stories began to gush and flow. I really had very few memories as I only spent about one week at Kirkham's. I just remember playing badminton there. However, my sister Ginny spent two years there so I took several photos to show her. I also enjoyed being with others to whom it was so dear.

Next was the Flach's residence on Inya Lake off of University Ave. We found it with no problem. The people who now lived there were French and were out shopping at the market. Their servants contacted them by phone (cell?) and we had permission to walk about the grounds. Edie says the place was in better shape than when her family lived there. We relived events that being there brought back to us. (I have to say that I think I spent more time at the Flach's, the Arce's and Johnnie Seymore's house than my home.) Butch showed where he, I, and Spike found the Japanese machine gun bullets. (That's another long story.)

The Flach house was maybe the best find in Rangoon (Yangon- I have to get used to calling it that.) for us. From there, we continued on to the Kokine Swimming Club. As kids, we probably spent more time here than anywhere else; it was the center of our daytime social life. Again, the roads looked different. Where there used to be jungle paths and basha huts now high rises and many more buildings were there, plus more roads and side streets. At the swimming club, it all looked the same. There were some minor changes, like a new pool behind where the old clubhouse was, and still is. The high dive had been removed. The 5-meter board is no longer there and the extended structure where Butch and I used to shimmy up about 10 meters where we dove off was missing. We met the treasurer of the club and told him how we practically lived there year round and he gave us each a key chain from the club. I was sorry that I didn't get one for Jerry and Ginny.

We then went to a government gem store, the only place that you can legally buy gems in Myanmar. I bought two necklaces of jade for my daughter Becky for a "song and a dance."

On to Chauk Htat Gyi Reclining Buddha, near the Kokine Swimming Club. The old Buddha image that my mother made an oil painting of was a huge structure in the jungle with only the head and torso still intact. It was centuries old and had trees growing out of cracks in the structure. I believe that the name meant "6 stories big." It no longer exists.

The new Chauk Htat Gyi looks like a golden ceramic reclining Buddha. It's a beautiful structure, but not as big as the original. (Or is that because when you are smaller, as I was then, things seem bigger?) This is said to be the largest Buddha image in Myanmar.

Sometime during this first day we drove by Joe and Mike Weil's compound and saw where they lived, and then we had lunch at a local Burmese restaurant. In the afternoon, we visited the Strand Hotel where Carolyn stayed for about six months and then to Bogyoke Market (also called Scotts market.) I remember going there when I was a teen, trying to sell some things that I received from the States, stuff like model airplanes and dope. (That's paint to put on the model airplanes.) This time I bought a sandalwood fan for Becky and a Shan bag for myself. We went to the Kandawgyi restaurant on Royal Lake for another glorious meal. Before going back to Winwin's, we went to the Inya Lake Sailing Club, (now called Yangon Sailing Club), where Edie had taken me for a moonlight sail back in 1957. Very romantic; I will never forget it. We could see the American embassy residence across the lake, where we spent many hours with the Kerr and Braddock families. We could also see the Flach residence at the south end of the lake. Sadly, we learned they no longer have moonlight sailing each month. Winwin joined us there for some appetizers and then we went back to the Kwong home. There we met some of Jai and Winwin's friends. They were important government people and local businessmen, very interesting to talk with and listen to.

Memories of Burma

Feb. 5, Saturday

After another fabulous breakfast at Winwin's, we were off to the Shwedagon Buddhist Temple. We arrived at the east gate, or entrance. Our guide was now Mr. Nyi, who remained with us for the rest of our stay in Myanmar. His English was excellent, and he was very polite, as are all Myanmar people. He was also very knowledgeable, and pleasant and liked to laugh a lot. I liked that. I told him my memory has it that there is a meadow and a pond at the north entrance of the Shwedagon. I asked him if that was so. Mr. Nyi said (as he said many times during our tours) that my memory was excellent as I continued to recall places, names and Burmese words. I told him that he should talk to the people I work with about my memory as they might disagree.

I think I remember these things because they were so vivid and important to me. As we walked around the base of the Shwedagon, I recalled that the height of the Shwedagon was 326 ft high. Again Mr. Nyi was surprised because that was exactly right. Why do I remember things like that from 47 years ago and can't remember what I had for dinner last night? As we toured the pagoda Mr. Nyi told us the meaning of many symbols such as a particular one that is associated with the day of the week you were born.

I am a rat. In Burmese mythology I think that's a good thing. I knew that Oliver was also a rat and sure enough, he is. Edie, also being born on Thursday is, however, a mouse (in my mind.) Lauri, born on a Saturday, is a dragon and Sue, born on Sunday, is a chiruda (man upper body and bird lower body.) I'm sorry that I didn't get the birthdays of the rest of the group, but I did buy a painting showing these symbols so we can figure out our symbols. Ginny has the painting.

Now here my memory failed me. We were given 45 minutes to go about on our own. I went to the south gate believing it was the major entrance to downtown Rangoon. I descended the many steps (hundreds it seemed) only to find I was wrong. I found out later it was the west entrance that I wanted, which we visited next. I bought a pair of sandals for myself and a teak wood carving for Ginny. I remember an old home movie that someone had taken of my mom and dad at the west entrance. It stands out because my dad was a tall man and stood well above the local people and you could pick him out so easily because of his height and blond hair.

Memories of Burma

The pair of sandals became important because every time we entered a temple, pagoda or private home, we were required to remove our foot wear. Sandals are easier to take off than laced tennis shoes and socks. The only time that I wore shoes and socks during the rest of the trip was when I was on an airplane.

There was another wonderful thing about Jai and Winwin's guide service. Traveling along with Mr. Nyi and the tour group was Mr. Tun. He spoke very little English but his job was to carry bags, open doors, pay tips when appropriate and pay for all meals and hotel expenses. He was also our banker. Whenever we needed Kyats, we'd tell how much we wanted and he would reach into his Shan bag, which was packed with bills and give us what we asked for, usually $100 worth. He'd then write it down in his journal. At the end of our stay, we would settle up with Winwin in American dollars. The arrangement was terrific for us.

After the Shwedagon, we drove around Royal Lake and saw Rangoon Technical High School, where my dad worked and taught. We didn't get to the back side where the Okalapa flats are situated, though I would have liked it as that's where we lived during our last year in Burma. The school was across the street from Aung San Park, which is still there, with a statue of General Aung San– still intact. He was the man who first led the resistance against British colonial rule which resulted eventually in Burma's independence in 1948. There is also a floating restaurant that looked like a golden ship, called Karaweik Hall.

Feb. 6, Sunday

We flew from Yangon to Mandalay with a brief stop in Bagan. It was about a one hour bus ride from the airport to the city because we stopped at a silk weaving factory, then visited and walked on U Bein Bridge (the world's longest bridge made entirely of teak wood.) I encountered a young girl who did her darndest to sell me a jade necklace. I finally broke down and bought it and we then became fast friends. I can still see her smile!!

Speaking of smiles, all you have to do in Myanmar to get a smile is to give one. Truly, to anyone, anytime, anywhere, I have never been disappointed. The same goes with a wave; they will always wave back if a hand is free. You must be careful though- a typical American wave would be to hold your arm up, hands palm out, and wave your palm up and down. Here, that's not a proper wave; it means "*laba laba*," "come here." In Myanmar, a side to side motion is best.

After the teak bridge, we went to a Buddhist Monastery, pronounced "Monastry." I guess that's the British influence. Here more than a thousand monks (I remember them as *Pongyis*), live and study. Nuns and initiates as young as eight live here as well. The old monks wore saffron robes, sometimes purple. The young initiates wore white, and the nuns, a pleasant shade of lavender.

After the monks entered in several single file rows to have their noonday meal (and final meal of the day), we were allowed to go inside the compound to visit and observe. Again, we left our shoes and socks outside the compound. Earlier, I had made the statement that I had used foresight by leaving my shoes in the bus and was wearing sandals while the others were stuck with more cumbersome footwear.

Meanwhile, Mr. Nyi and I talked to a monk who knew and was associated with some monks that I had met at a Buddhist temple in Boulder Creek, California in 2001. I had a lengthy and interesting conversation with him. When I went back to the street where I had left my sandals, they weren't there! This was unheard of. No one steals someone's sandals! But, they weren't where I had left them. I began to doubt my memory and I looked several places before I found them in the middle of the street, quite a ways from where I left them. Then it dawned on me. All I had to do was look at Oliver's innocent face to realize that my smug declaration about the sandals was the source of this prank. Throughout the trip, the two of us continued to pull pranks on each other, though Oliver always had the upper hand. He has a devious mind. What a guy!

I want to say here that I noticed that all the monks seemed to be in really good physical shape; none were fat. Must be the diet and exercise they do during the day.

We had lunch at another restaurant in Mandalay. We then checked into the Sedona Hotel which was across the street from the ancient palace where King Thebaw lived with the royal family until they were deposed by the British in the late 1800's. ("The Glass Palace" by Amitav Ghosh is a great read for anyone who is interested in this part of Myanmar's history.)

Memories of Burma

The palace is surrounded by a moat that appears to be about one mile long on each of four sides. That evening, we visited the hill above Mandalay to view the city at sunset. There we met a large group of teenagers who were in a private school, learning to speak English. They were very anxious to practice on us so we talked for a long time. Earlier we had visited another temple that had been made entirely of teak wood. It had been built in the 16th century. The temple had been moved during the war to protect it. So much history! I asked Mr. Nyi if any temples or shrines had been damaged during WWII and was told that the Japanese, being Buddhists, avoided damaging religious structures. Back at the hotel (where earlier Randy and I went for a swim in the hotel pool), Randy, Diane, Allen and I went for a walk in search of "The Green Elephant Restaurant." We never found it, so we came back to the hotel to go to the Uno Lounge to receive our "welcome drink."

Randy, Diane and I went to the 4th floor lounge in search of a martini before turning in. Diane told me that had been her mother's favorite drink in Burma. Turns out, the bartender had no idea how to make one. We still hadn't had dinner so we also ordered a pizza. At least an hour went by before we finally got the pizza but still no martini. When it finally arrived it turns out to be pure Martini-Rossi vermouth. Oh well, to bed.

Feb. 7, Monday

We took a boat trip up the Irawaddy River to Mingun, an ancient, unfinished pagoda. The king who started the construction died before it was finished and construction was stopped. Only the base remains. The beginning of the boat ride was quite extraordinary, as our boat was surrounded by at least a half dozen other boats. We appeared to be in a log jam. As we watched, the owners and captains of the surrounding boats moved and maneuvered, all working together. It must have been an every day occurrence as although it looked confusing, it didn't take long to untangle. We boarded the boat by going from one vessel to another while walking on wooden planks and using a hand rail that was a wooden shaft held at each end by two seamen. The boat ride was pleasant, and after about forty-five minutes we were met by oxcarts to take us to the temple. I bought a straw hat to keep the sun from my bald spot. I had been using a St. Louis Cardinals baseball cap that Bill loaned me. When we got to the temple, I couldn't find the baseball cap. By the time I found it, the group was going back to the boat so I didn't get to see that temple.

Memories of Burma

We returned to Mandalay where we visited a tapestry and puppet factory and then went to lunch. We went to a restaurant that we never would have picked on our own; we walked down a dirty and unkempt alley to a back-door-type place. We ordered Burmese curry and it was great! Local knowledge and another great find by the fabulous Mr. Nyi. Our "banker" Mr. Tun was also in charge of a special piece of luggage. It was actually a large chest that turned out to be a wine locker that Oliver and Susan had shipped to accompany our travels. Inside were at least a dozen bottles of exquisite and expensive wines. What a special treat. Upon request, Mr. Tun would produce a few bottles and joy would prevail! We shared these wines at several meals as we did at this one in this obscure restaurant in Mandalay. Thanks so much Oliver and Susan!

We went back to the hotel where Bill and I relaxed at the pool while Randy and Allen went to a book store and the others went shopping. That evening we went to do some more shopping at jade and marble carving shops as well as silk and fabric weavers. Then we went to a comedy club called the "Moustache Brothers." The show may have been better if we weren't all so tired and anxious to get back to the hotel. However, when the comedian's wife came on stage to dance, it was great. She was a great dancer of Burmese style. She also was accompanied by two ladies who were good. (Not as good as the wife, but good none the less.) So, the dancers carried the show. It almost went on too long, but we all agreed it was worth seeing.

Feb. 8, Tuesday

We left Mandalay for the airport where we would fly to Heho. We were totally delighted to see Jai and meet Mei, who was already on board. This was the first time I had seen Mei since 1958 and she was then *Mei Mei*, or "little sister," as she was ten years old. What a terrific lady, so beautiful and with a ready smile.

At Heho we took a one hour bus ride to the jetty where we were to take a boat ride across Inle Lake to our hotel. On the way to the jetty, we stopped to take some pictures of fishermen fishing and also some water buffalo on the side of the road. The buffalo seemed to be in an argument over something, as they had locked horns. Oliver noticed that as soon as we stopped and got out of the bus, they quit fighting. He said that they must have known we were the boss and decided to behave.

Memories of Burma

At the jetty, we boarded three five-man boats. They reminded me of long dugouts, probably 15 feet long with a strange outboard motor on the back. The boats had a kind of elongated shaft to the prop. You'd have to see a picture to understand. It was about a one hour boat ride to the Khaung Dine hotel, a magnificent place with a gate for an entrance set out on a bay of the lake. It was surrounded by "floating huts" that were the individual rooms on stilts in the bay.

We were assigned rooms at dockside. Lauri and Carolyn were given the "Queen's Suite," Jai and Mei the "Princess Suite," and Randy and I, the "Prince Suite," all on the hillside overlooking the water. The others were in the "floating huts" on the lake. At first I was jealous not to be on the water but then we noticed that the floating huts all had mosquito netting above the beds, while ours' on the hillside didn't. As it turned out we didn't see a mosquito while there anyway. It must have been the right time of the year.

We then took a boat ride to Indein village and took a long walk up a hillside and through a village and market place where I bought a shirt on the way back. At the end of our climb, we saw a centuries-old complex of shrines and stupas. It must have been an archaeologist's dream. Hundreds of old shrines, most in disrepair, pieces of carved stones lying about on the ground everywhere. You'd have to see photos to realize the extent of the place. It was totally unreal- an Indiana Jones scene comes to mind.

The walk between the boat and the temples was through a dense bamboo forest. It was an amazing place. Back in our boats, we saw many fisherman and "leg paddlers" on our way back to the hotel.

Feb. 9, Wednesday

We took a boat ride across to the east side of Inle Lake. First, we went to a pre-school for local children. They must have known we were coming, as they had a program prepared for us. They sang and danced. We gave them prepared gifts of school supplies and some candy. The Flach family sang a song for them in Burmese called *Pojo*, or "old man." Fun was had by all.

From the school we went to a market, kind of like the Milpitas, California flea market. I noticed that Jai and Mei kept a close eye on me or at least helped me make intelligent purchases. They must have thought that I looked like a kid in a candy store. I love them!

Memories of Burma

At one point I figured out how to become invisible. I squatted down on the ground like a local and just watched. It worked. Mei took a lot of movies and snapshots. I hope I get a chance to see them.

We returned to the school and had another show put on by the kids as they were practicing for a dance and song competition. We made a financial contribution and left with a grand feeling inside.

We took another half hour boat ride to a floating restaurant where we were welcomed by a group of musicians playing drums and gongs. Again, we were being treated like royalty. We had lunch on the deck overlooking the waterway entrance to the restaurant. Mei and Jai selected our dishes and as usual everything was superb. It was time to leave, and my group and I were boarding the boat; the musicians began to play again. Noticing that they didn't play for other boats leaving, Oliver said, "It looks like they are very happy to see you go, Dave!" As we motored out of the bay, I realized that a new boat was arriving, causing the music. Another round for Oliver!

Memories of Burma

Our next stop was Phaung Daw Oo Pagoda, a pagoda featuring five Buddha heads. The story is that these five heads were being transported to the temple when a big storm blew up and one head was lost overboard. Sometime later (I'm not sure how long) the fifth head showed up along side the others all draped in seaweed. It's believed to be a miracle. This all happened several centuries ago, I believe.

We visited a silk weaving factory and a cigar making factory, all on stilt teak wood shops on the lake. Then we took a one hour boat ride back to the jetty where we started from two days before and got back on the bus.

All of these excursions had been planned and carried out by Mr. Nyi. Our group only had to follow instructions. It was so easy to comply.

It was now getting close to evening and Jai changed plans as he wanted to show us the city of Taungyi. This is an ancient capitol city where Jai and Mei and family would vacation during the hot summer days as Taungyi is located high in the cool Shan hills. The Kwong family had close friendships with Shan royalty so they would spend the sweltering days in cool weather. I'm so glad that we were able to see Taungyi rather than just be told about it, although it was almost dark when we drove through and we didn't see as much as we would have liked.

We soon arrived at our next hotel, the Aye Thar Golf Resort Hotel. Jerry and Kay would have liked it here. It looked like a fine golf course, but we arrived at dark and left early the next morning so didn't see much of the grounds. The patrons are, of course, businessmen and generals so a lot of business and government policy is decided here. Just like in the States. Mr. Nyi mentioned that a round of golf costs about $10 in Myanmar.

It was now the evening of the ninth of February, which was Chinese New Year. So we celebrated "Kung Hay Fat Choy" at the restaurant. It had been a long day and all were tired and off to our individual bungalows. The last to leave the restaurant were Jai, Mei, Bill, Edie, Randy and myself. The six of us plus a driver rode a golf cart to our rooms which looked like a Burmese bus with people hanging on the outside and holding on top. Someone took a picture, and I hope I get to see it.

Memories of Burma

Feb. 10, Thursday

On to Bagan by plane and lunch at Riverside Sunset Garden Restaurant. We had a quick swim at the hotel pool and were on to more temple viewing. Now, this is the most incredible place for ancient temples in all of Myanmar. We were off to visit these magnificent temples.

I need to stop my travelogue here for an observation: everywhere we stopped we were surrounded by merchants. They were usually children, and as their parents must know, hard to resist. As they tried to sell their wares, the typical pitch is, "Hello, hello, lucky money, lucky money." (They say this in English of course). As we stepped off the bus, it seemed that most of the vendors made a bee line straight for me and followed me everywhere I go, calling their chant followed by, "How much you pay?" Once we arrived at an agreed price, it's, "Good for you and good for me," and everyone is happy. If I went and paid the original price, I'm sure that they would have been disappointed. Now, if I didn't buy, they followed me up to the bus and as I sat there trying to ignore them, they rapped on the window and used sign language to try to make a last sale. Some of the guys and gals in our group said that they can spot a soft touch easily. Edie and Lauri claimed it's because I am such a "nice guy."

Someone else (I don't recall who - O.F. maybe) says I've got "sucker" written on my forehead. I think it's more because I'm interested in people, make eye contact, and love to stop and chat with them. I like to see them smile.

Then it was off to a sunset at another pagoda overlooking the Irawaddy River. Magnificent! As we were waiting for the sunset (which was so magnificent each evening, almost like a sunset seen nowhere else; more reddish, more exotic than I can remember ever seeing anywhere else, only Burma!), many children were trying to sell us trinkets. Oliver and Susan handled it really well. I overheard what they were up to. They said, "Hey guys, can you keep a secret? Yes? O.K. Here's the secret: I'll buy a group of postcards from each of you for 500 kyats each, but you'll have to promise that you won't try to sell us, any of us, any more cards. Now, do we have a deal? They agreed and Oliver and Susan gave them the money. But it wasn't long before they tried again. When they came to me I said, "You promised." I got a look that said that they didn't know I was part of the deal. So I tried another tactic. I showed them my wiggly eye trick and they showed me how to "snap" my fingers and soon we were buddies. I asked them their ages, which were 15 to 17 years old, and asked them to guess mine. The boldest one said,

"67?" After a pause, I said, "Close enough". All these children are so handsome and beautiful. It brings joy to the heart.

We went to another major temple called the Shwezigon, and I gave a few cheroots to a policeman. He was now my friend and following us on our tour. Oliver noticed this and told me to give him some kyats when I could do it discretely to cement our relationship. Now we really were buddies and I didn't even get arrested for bribing a policeman. I think that Oliver was hoping for more fireworks than that.

Feb. 11, Friday

This morning was a blur of more temples and more markets. At one temple, I decided to buy a painting and another Shan bag. Then, instead of viewing temples, I decided to play with the kids who were trying to sell stuff. Oliver had given me a handful of rubber bands and soon the children weren't merchants anymore, but children- just like me. I took off my straw hat, set it on a bicycle seat and four boys, one girl and myself had a contest trying to knock the hat off with rubber bands. I lost of course, because they cheated. I had drawn a line in the dirt about 10 feet from the target but they kept

Memories of Burma

shooting from "point blank range" of about one foot. Again, I showed them my wiggly eye trick and we parted as friends.

At lunch we saw an exceptional puppet show, which went on forever with lots of curtain calls. I think that Carolyn especially liked it as she got a special hug from the performers who found out her fondness for horses which were a major part of the show.

We then went for a pony cart ride to another glorious sunset, back to the Tharabah Gate Hotel in Bagan for dinner where we met another of Jai's friends. This was our final night in Bagan, and our dinner companions were U Saw Weik and his wife Htay Htay. U Saw was at one time the government's leading guide for the archeological finds at Bagan. He is now a private businessman and owns a guide service. He and Htay Htay are perhaps the most knowledgeable people on Bagan history, geology and architecture in the country and it was extremely interesting listening to them. Altogether, it was a very worthwhile evening.

Feb. 12, Saturday

We returned to Yangon by Air Bagan. I got autographs from two flight attendants who were featured in the airlines magazine. Air Bagan is one of only three private airlines in the country, and it's only a few years old. We noticed that there was a supervisor on board giving O.J.T. (on the job training), to the flight crew. We asked where she was from and she replied, "It's a long story, but Turkey." Diane noticed the logo on the tray tables were Air Mexico.

Back in Yangon, we went to the Dusit Inya Lake Hotel that was built by the Russians back in 1958 or so. It's a first class place, very beautiful, and overlooked the lake.

Bill, Edie, Lauri, Susan and I borrowed a car from Winwin's fleet and went looking for more old homes in Rangoon. Unfortunately, the one my family lived in on Kokine Road (now Kaba Aye Pagoda Road) was gone, replaced by high rises and commercial buildings. But we did find what we think was Chichi and Roberto's home. The servants of the owners allowed us to take photographs of it and we'll have to check with the Arces to see if it was their home.

We went on to Chin Tsong Avenue and looked for Bill Ramlow's first home, which we didn't find. I remember a story about a tennis court and a Burmese python, which I'll tell later. But we did get some great pictures of the

Memories of Burma

Kambawja palace where we all lived for many months while waiting for a home to move into. We did find Bill's second home, right on University Avenue. We then found what we thought was Betsy and Bruce Lindeman's house on old Windemere road. I remember many parties there.

We went back to Winwin's for a silver and gem cocktail party. I bought some silver baskets for Mary and the girls bought some ruby and sapphire rings.

Then we saw a *pwe* dance show at poolside, where professional Myanmar dancers performed. As was customary, we each presented envelopes of cash to the dancers of our choice, provided by Jai of course. At Winwin's house this night, Mei gave me a gift; a picture book of photographs by three Myanmar photographers. The book is called "Myanmar Smiles" and Mei said she bought two copies; one for herself and one for me, because she said that I was so sensitive to people of other cultures. Also, I like people who smile. I treasure this book. Mei, I'll love you forever.

Then back to Inya Lake too tired for more than a drink when the mosquitoes drove us inside for bedtime.

Memories of Burma
Feb. 13, Sunday

We were joined at breakfast by Jai, Winwin and Mei, where we finalized our accounts and boarded the bus for the final trip to the airport at Mingaladon. We waved goodbye and were gone. The last I saw the Kwongs was on the front steps of the Dusit Hotel.

Fortunately for us, Mei was flying to Bangkok with us. I say "fortunate," because the Yangon Airport was a fiasco, jammed with travelers all trying to get through customs at the same time. Mei took charge and got our group all through, in what seemed like an hour or so. She even handled passports and seat assignments for all but Randy who was scheduled to fly out the next day and thought he would try on standby. The last we saw him he was at the gate waiting. Never saw him again. I'll have to write to Diane and find out what happened. I'll have to say that he was a great roommate and a pleasure to travel with. So long, Rangoon!

We landed at Bangkok airport and here our group went different ways. Mei, Edie, Lauri, Susan and Oliver were going on to Hong Kong. Bill was headed to L.A. by way of Seoul, Korea (I think), and Joe and Caroline and I were flying on United to Japan where we parted. I was going to San Francisco, and they were going to Denver by way of Seattle. Carolyn was headed to Detroit by way of Seattle on the next morning's flight. She left at 6 am, and I at 7 am. We strolled around the Amorie hotel and I did some shopping where I bought a chess set for my son Matt and a carved incense burner for my daughter Becky. Had a light dinner and to bed as we needed to get up at about three in the morning for our flights.

Feb. 14, Monday

I met Joe and Caroline at the gate and we were only a row and a seat apart on our way to Japan, so that was comforting for me. At Narita, I went into the executive lounge as their guest, so had a comfortable wait for my final flight to San Francisco. Thanks, Joe and Caroline, for your help. I was able to bring back some wonderful Myanmar arts and craft souvenirs which reflect the culture and traditions of the country and its people.

I'm now home in time for Valentine's Day. It's going to take me several days to fight off jet lag. I'm so glad that I went - what an experience!!!

So this last reunion is like a completed circle. Those of us who weren't able to go were not forgotten as we traveled around and shared new experiences. I intend to send this letter to those who might enjoy what we did knowing that we were thinking of you all.

P.S.: Lauri brought to my attention some things we noticed in Myanmar. Good things. Pleasant changes. Remember the hoards of *pye* (pie) dogs that roamed the streets? We saw very few of those and those we did see were in pretty good condition. Also, in Rangoon there were very few of those old decrepit buses jam-packed with people inside and on top. We did see these buses, cars, and trucks outside of Rangoon, however. There were no jeep taxis circling Independence Square and far fewer trishaws (I remember them as "si-cars", or side cars.) I also noticed that there were no beggars and sick people on the streets looking for handouts. Also, the city was clean. There weren't many betel nut stains on the ground, and I don't recall any intrusive smells. The Shwedagon was especially clean. We were no longer bothered by walking barefoot on the tiles around the pagoda. One thing hasn't changed though – the friendly attitude of the Burmese people.

Memories of Burma

Two phrases we used every day:

Mingalaba - Hello

Ce-zu-tin-ba-deh – Thank You

Mei and Jai Kwong at Indein Village near Inle Lake

Bagan temples

Mei and local children at Indein Village

Kambawja Hotel in Rangoon

Shwedagon pagoda from across Royal Lake in Rangoon

Memories of Burma

David at Inle Lake

Fisherman at Inle Lake

Memories of Burma

Reunion group at Mandalay. Glass Palace in background.

Winwin's home in Rangoon

Burma Memories

Rangoon, June of 1956, during a monsoon rain storm

As we arrived at the Mingladon airport in Rangoon and disembarked from our flight, we were met by a surprise welcoming group of young people. Some of them were Americans but also other kids from different nationalities. As we found out later, the Embassy would contact the international community whenever a new family with children was arriving and their children would come to greet the incoming families to welcome them to Rangoon. The "children" would be of the ages between 8 and 20.

The airport at Mingladon was located about 10 miles from Rangoon so we took taxis to our hotel. The hotel where our family was booked was the Kambawja Hotel—also known as the Chin Tsong palace. It was situated in a beautiful jungle garden and its architecture was from the 1700's or so. It was called the Chin Tsong Palace because it was built for/by a Chinese prince of that name. Now in 1956, had been converted into a beautiful hotel. It had a dining area in the center beneath a three story domed ceiling with individual living quarters located in wings off to the side. By the way, my family consisted of dad, mom, my brother Jerry (16), sister Ginny (10) and myself (14).

The hotel was to be our home for several months until we found a house to move into. The place was like an oriental castle. My introduction to Asia was dreamlike, mysterious and intriguing. The hotel was not on the main road but had an entrance guarded by stone pillars, a metal gate and a sweeping driveway that crossed over a pond before reaching the hotel entrance. We loved being there as there were other "Europeans" also staying there and we began to build friendships and bonds.

The weather in Burma was very hot and humid, especially during the monsoon season which began in late May and extended until late August. There was no air conditioning, but each unit and every residence had ceiling fans to cool the air.

Each day a driver of one or another of the embassy people would collect us kids at the hotel and bring us to their residences where we would be entertained and could mix with others our age. We were becoming part of the international family of Burma.

Every Friday night there would be a chaperoned party at one of the residences. Most of the international community was American. However, the party also included those from other countries; Sweden, Denmark, China, Yugoslavia, Israel, Australia, England, Bolivia, India, and Indonesia just to name a few. Our parents and the embassy personnel kept us constantly entertained. We lived the life of princes and princesses.

Eventually we found a place to move into. It was a compound surrounded by an eight foot wall for security. There were two homes in the compound; another American family in one home and my family in the other.

Once we moved from the hotel to our new home it became clear that we needed servants in order to exist in this society. Our family hired a cook to buy food from the local market and prepare our everyday meals. Since we didn't have decent refrigeration we needed to buy food every day for that day's meals. We didn't speak the language and at the market one needed to bargain for each item. The price was automatically inflated by at least 10 times when any foreigner tried to purchase anything at the market. No—we needed a local agent to do the purchase, hence the cook.

We hired a nanny to look after us kids, do the house work and help with the meals. The nanny, Sein Sein, was like a second mother to us. She was also the wife of the cook. Sein Sein was with us for our entire stay in Burma, about two years. Her name translated into English means "diamond of diamonds." She truly lived up to her name.

Dad also hired a Mahli (gardener) to take care of the compound, which was a daily job. In South East Asia, one has to cut the lawn, trim the vegetation and rid the area of unwanted "critters" each day. Burma is a lush, tropical, area where you could clear a path in the jungle and a few days later it would be overgrown. Lawn mowers were non-existent so the lawn was cut using a machete being slapped horizontally on the ground in a sweeping motion.

We also hired a Durwan (night watchman). This was necessary because once it was known that a compound is being guarded by a Durwan the likelihood of a robbery diminished. The more fierce the reputation of your Durwan, the better protection you had. I recall that our watchman had allegedly once killed someone. True or untrue, who knows? But his reputation preceded him. He was a Sikh from the Punjabi states of northern India, a tribe known as fierce warriors. The best protection money could buy. We were never, ever, robbed!

Our final servant was our driver, Maung Gyi. Since there was no telephone service in Rangoon outside of the main government offices (of which we were not a part) all communication between private parties was done by hand written messages delivered by the driver. Maung Gyi was also responsible, first and foremost, for bringing dad to and from work and any other appointments that he had. He also drove each of our family members to any events when he was free to do so.

Obviously each of our servants spent a great deal of time every day looking after our needs.

The Kambawja Hotel in Rangoon

Good friends at a typical Friday night party at the Olson's home

From the left: David Olson, the author, Sally Lou Arnold, the daughter of the director of the Ford Foundation sponsoring the Rangoon Technical High school where David's dad worked, Phoebe Thirkield, daughter of a U.S. Naval officer attached to the U.S Embassy, and Vlado Marusic, son of the Yugoslavian Ambassador.

Up On the Roof

Our new home on Kokine Road was a two story Spanish style adobe structure. We could walk up to the third floor, which was the roof surrounded by a waist high retaining wall, that would allow us to spend quiet evenings overlooking the compound and also facing the main road. One night I was on the roof alone. It was a spectacular evening, quite warm and with a full moon. Suddenly, a shadow of something crossed over the roof. Looking up I was startled to see what looked like a gigantic bat flying overhead, backlit by the light of the moon. Since no one was there to see it but me, I ran downstairs yelling for others to come to the roof. My parents thought that I was exaggerating and my brother thought it was my imagination because of course, when they came to look, there was no giant bat. I couldn't convince them as the story seemed so absurd. Each time I told the bat story, the bat grew in size to a four or five foot wing span. We had only been in Asia a few months and we were still trying to get used to the mysterious environment, culture and exotic wildlife. Everything was a new adventure.

Several days later, while talking with our cook and the Mahli, they said "oh sure, there's a family of fruit bats living in the tree by the road in front of the house." These mammals are also known as flying foxes because of their size, grow quite large and have a wing span of up to six feet. The bats are total vegetarians, eating mostly fruit and only flying at night. At first my introduction to the bats was, kind of scary, but I was glad to know that I wasn't just "seeing things."

Our first home at 51A Kokine Road

Breakfast with a Cobra

For meals, our cook would bring food from the cook house to us seated in the dining room. Maung Tein was always smiling and appeared to be so proud of each meal as if he considered it a unique creation. The cook house was located separately from the main house connected by a covered walkway of about fifteen steps.

One morning he wasn't smiling. As we were waiting for breakfast, we heard a loud yell followed by a crash coming from the cook house corridor. Then a lot more yelling and crashing noises that we assumed was our breakfast hitting the floor. Maung Tein finally screamed in English "SNAKE, SNAKE." It turned out that as he came out toward the dining area, he'd come face to face with a King Cobra, right in the middle of the walkway. This was enough to stop even the bravest heart. He was fortunate that he wasn't bitten.

The yelling alerted the other servants who brought long sticks that they used to move the cobra from the house and into the compound yard.

Now the real pandemonium began. All the servants, their families, children, wives, husbands and friends came. They settled into a circle around the area where the cobra was being held captive distracted by several men who showed bravery using long bamboo poles to poke at the snake. The snake's long neck held its head erect, swiveling in confusion from side to side as the creature tried to detect where the next threat was coming from.

Thus began a day of partying by everyone from both homes in the compound. No more work was accomplished that day as this was an unusual event for all. A circus atmosphere developed. Word got out to the nearby community and soon our compound was crowded with neighbors and sightseers. Street vendors arrived selling food and local snacks.

Eventually, a man arrived who had a pet mongoose, a natural enemy of the cobra. The mongoose was tethered on a leash and the snake and the mongoose then engaged in an epic battle.

Normally the mongoose will win this fight as it will push its nose to within striking distance of the snake. As the snake strikes, the mongoose, with lightning speed jumps either to the side, straight up or to the rear and out of danger. Once the snake has struck and is extended it is vulnerable. This is when the mongoose will grab the snake behind the head and kill it. The owner however yanked the leash to keep the snake from being killed and the battle continued. I didn't see the end of the show but I have to assume that the snake was eventually the loser.

That was not the end of the party as it continued throughout the day and well into the night. Brother Jerry, sister Ginny and I were still sitting out behind the servants' quarters well past midnight watching as the still partying locals passed around what we assumed was an opium pipe. A total holiday and an unforgettable event.

Nats

Burmese culture includes a belief in supernatural beings called Nats. They are the spirits of people who have died untimely deaths, either by accident or violence. The locals believe that Nats can influence or interfere with the living.

Coming from a western society as we did, we didn't think there was much truth to this notion. However, as children we were more receptive to local beliefs and ideas.

I mentioned our house was a two story building. The first floor was a living and dining area, the bedrooms on the second floor. The stairway continued to the roof where we could open a door and step out onto the veranda-like roof.

My mother, Maxine, would often go downstairs at night to get a soft drink, then bring it upstairs to her room and read for a while. One night I awoke, as I heard someone walking up the stairs. The footsteps didn't end at the second floor but continued onto the roof. I heard the door open and close. Thinking this was my mom going to the roof to enjoy the evening and her drink, I got out of bed to join her.

When I stepped onto the roof, I realized that I was alone. Mom was not there, no one was there. I had distinctly heard footsteps, the door open and close, but no one was there. Was this just a dream or the result of an overactive teenage imagination? Everything seemed so real that to this day it seems as though things really happened as I remember.

Our cook always had many stories that he told us kids and I believed all of them. He believed that someone had been killed in this house and that it was the Nat who had walked to the roof that night. He claimed that I noticed the Nat because I was so receptive to the spirits. I've come to believe that there are some things that happen in Asia that oppose what we Western folks consider reality but may have a truth all of its own.

Memories of Burma

Ginny's Story

Author's note: The following section was sent to me by my sister Ginny in 2010.

I was only 10 when we went to Burma. By we, I mean my two teenage brothers Jerry and David, and my parents. Before we went I was pretty exited but decided to bargain with my dad about going. I said I would only go if I could have a horse. Hey, I was ten! A horse! Well, we went anyway.

I guess my first memory of when we arrived in Rangoon was the smell. Rangoon!! What a great sounding word. I was too young to really understand anything romantic, but I must have had some adolescent sense of romance and RANGOON was definitely special in some way, of which I wasn't quite sure yet. Oh, back to the smell. It was the fish market and it was overwhelming. I don't remember exactly when the smell disappeared for me and the beauty of the country began. But it did eventually.

The first place we lived when we arrived was at the Kambawja Palace. It was kind of a hotel. I have some vague memory one night of standing up in the middle of the dining room in the palace where all the guests were eating dinner and announcing to every one there that all of our vegetables were grown from human manure. Oh dear. My parents were mortified. I guess I must have been punished for this but I don't remember. I guess I was a difficult child sometimes. A few days into our stay at the palace, my dad and I went on a walk. We walked past a small hut, where a man and his daughter were living. They invited us in and were so gracious and offered us tea. I remember talking to the little girl who was about my age and asking her what grade she was in. I was so proud that I was in a higher grade even though we were the same age. It is a memory that later I was not proud of because of my arrogance. There is so much to learn about the differences of people of different cultures.

I don't really remember how long we stayed at the Kambawja Palace, but one day we moved to a house. I have to explain this house, because here in the states it would be quite unusual. We lived in a compound consisting of two homes, a few huts, and about four garages with servants' quarters above the garages. The entire compound was surrounded by a gate which was locked at night. In the states you live in a house. In Rangoon you live in a compound where many people congregate at all times, every day. I can't ever remember being bored or lonely there. There was always someone around. People you didn't know who were probably related to the servants who lived there or maybe

Memories of Burma

not. It didn't matter. It was exciting.

I have to tell about a time when I went to a party at the mahli's house. A mahli was a gardener. He lived in a hut in the back of our compound. He was from someplace in India. I don't know where exactly, except that he was very large, wore a turban on his head and wrapped his body in some kind of cloth around his groin area. I think he might have worn sandals too. Anyhow, I was sitting in his hut one night watching his guests smoking something funny smelling from a pipe when my father suddenly came in and grabbed me and pulled me out of the party. I guess the mahli was having a party where everyone was smoking opium. A ten year old girl at an opium party!

One day I was walking to a neighbor's house who lived in our compound. I suddenly stopped as I was confronted by a cobra about ten feet away, sitting straight up looking at me with his head hooded. Oh boy, the only snake I had ever seen in Minnesota was a garden snake that was kind of cute. This was not cute. I wasn't sure what to do but I thought being quiet was a good idea. So, I very carefully backed away from the snake until I felt safe and then ran like the dickens to the servants' quarters and told them all about my encounter. I don't think anyone believed me as when they came to look, no cobra was hanging around waiting to

Memories of Burma

be captured. I have heard a story that our compound had a great party sometime later involving a mongoose and a bunch of people poking sticks at the cobra. This is not my memory, but who knows I was probably off to other adventures by then.

My father was an instructor and was sent to live in Burma by the Ford Foundation. A school was built by the foundation and my dad was in charge of training the electrical department. On the day of dedication of the school to the government, it was decided that I was to give a bouquet of flowers to the Prime Minister of Burma, U Nu. In a special ceremony, I was given the huge bouquet to carry on the stage in front of hundreds of guests. Unfortunately, no one told me what the Prime Minister looked like. So, I gave the bouquet to the wrong person. Fortunately everyone laughed and the real Prime Minister U Nu graciously accepted the bouquet later.

In the spring there is a celebration called the Water Festival. I think it is in May just before the monsoons begin. It gets pretty crazy and people spray each other with water all over the city. We had great fun in front of our house stopping cars and spraying people with buckets of water. Our house was a two story house with a flat roof on top you could access from some steps.

Memories of Burma

Every morning our cook and sweeper (house keeper/nanny) would enter the house by the door by the kitchen in order to prepare breakfast. One morning, I decided I was going to spray the cook and sweeper with a bucket of water as they unlocked the kitchen door. So, I had my bucket of water ready and was waiting above the kitchen door on the roof. This apparently was a special Buddhist morning, where the cook and sweeper were all dressed up in their finest clothes and were going to temple after breakfast. They were so proud of the way they looked. Unfortunately as they unlocked the door, I dumped a huge bucket of water on them, ruining their special clothes. Our cook chased me all over the house and was told by my parents that it was okay to spank me, which he readily accepted.

My girlfriends and I took Indian dancing from someone we called BaBoo. I always thought that was his name until years later I learned it meant "teacher" in Hindi. We used to take the lessons at the home of my friend whose father was the Charge d'Affair of Burma. It was a beautiful home with a huge veranda in back overlooking Inya Lake. We were told we (my two friends and I) would be dancing for a number of ambassadors one evening on the veranda. I don't know who all the VIPs were, but I know one was the Russian Ambassador. There is part of the dance where in the semi-dark, we are dressed in our saris on our knees with plates on our heads and lit candles on the plates, and we must pick up handkerchiefs with our mouths from the floor without dropping the plates. One friend had trouble picking up the napkin, as it had fallen flat, so the other friend and I had to wait with our heads down to the floor, with lit candles on the plates, with a napkin in our mouths for a couple of minutes (it seemed much longer) until my friend's napkin was propped up enough for her to grasp it. I remember getting a standing ovation from all the ambassadors. I will never forget that moment.

    I would like to tell the story about me making cheroots and smoking them with the servants one night, but I'm tired now and think I'll go to bed. After all I'm no longer ten and can't stay up getting into mischief anymore. Maybe I'll tell this story in the sequel to this book, David.

Ginny

Memories of Burma

Ginny in the middle

From the back: Carolyn Bacon, Ginny Olson (young blond girl), Phoebe Thirkield, Judy Carpenter, Sally Lou Arnold, and Carolyn Braddock

The Mahli

The Water Festival

In Southeast Asia there are only two seasons; the dry season and the wet season. The dry season begins about the end of August and continues until mid April or early May. This is when the monsoons begin. We experienced rain storms almost every day. This was considered to be a joyous time as it signals the beginning of the growing season. The celebration of the Water Festival precedes the beginning of the monsoons.

It is a three day celebration that originally began with people armed with a cup of water and a twig, usually something fragrant like sandalwood. The twig would be dipped into the water and then drops were sprinkled onto another's shoulder while wishing them a happy and prosperous wet season.

Over the years the festivals evolved into a wilder event with the revelers throwing cold buckets of water on anyone who ventured into the streets. There were a few groups of people who were exempt from the soakings. It was taboo to throw water on pregnant women, on Buddhist monks and most importantly, on soldiers or policemen. After all, these were people with guns. You didn't want to anger them. Often, being drenched with water—at least to us kids—was not unwelcome because at this time of the year the temperature would go into the 100's and it didn't take long to dry off.

Things tended to get quite wild at times. Kokine Road, which ran in front of our home, was the main thoroughfare from Rangoon. The road ran north to the airport and continued on to Mandalay in northern Burma. It was a very busy road with a lot of traffic.

We hooligans would wait until a bus was coming and stop it by placing a barricade across the road. Once stopped, we would run onto it splashing water on the riders as we ran through the front door and exiting at the rear. Then we removed the barrier and waited for the next bus to repeat our assault. If we were youths today and tried this in our current time here in the States, we would undoubtedly spend a lot of time in juvenile hall. We weren't alone, as youngsters throughout the country were being just as rowdy as we.

The next day, those of us that I refer to as the internationals (the children of embassy personnel), hired a large flatbed truck on which we placed a 55 gallon drum filled with water used to fill our water guns. The "guns" were bicycle pumps that we would use to squirt water at our targets as we rode around Rangoon doing water battle with others also armed with water devices. There were about fifteen of us on the truck and we were having fun being in the moment.

All was not always pleasant, however. I recall some of the locals yelled at us as they thought that as foreigners we didn't belong in the festival. One epitaph that I vividly remember was "Johnnie Walker—go home." That was a term used for English people. They thought we were English and there was a lingering dislike of the British colonization of Burma that had begun in about 1870 or so. Although there were a couple of English children in our group, we were after all just children.

Once we had to stop to refill our barrel at a local well and I got into some serious trouble. As I got off the truck to fill a pail, several people upended me into the well. When I came to the surface, people surrounding the well began to beat my head with pots and pans. Almost immediately however, my assailants began tumbling into the well. Hands reached down to help me to safety. My saviors were friends from our truck, Chichi and his brother Roberto. My Bolivian friends probably saved me from serious injury by hurtling my attackers into the well and pulling me out.

I'm sure that the excitement of the time was what fueled the attack, plus the misidentification of being English when the English were not well liked as it was less than ten years since Burma had gotten it's independence from England.

At that time, Americans were regarded as heroes in Burma as their efforts to drive the Japanese invasion forces out of the country were still fresh in the minds of the Burmese people, so their anger at us during the festival was misdirected.

With the exception of that one incident, my recall of the Water Festival was exciting and enjoyable. It was just another day in living a great adventure.

A scene from the Water Festival

Kokine Swimming Club

The Kokine Swimming Club was the center of our daytime social life. As kids, we spent hours at the pool—swimming for fun and trying to stay cool during the hot summer days while competing for trophies and prizes offered by the club officers to keep us entertained. We had contests in swimming, diving and one of the national sports, water polo.

Each embassy would provide a team of adults to compete for the water polo championship. I don't recall which embassy was dominant because they didn't stand a chance against us teenagers. We were made up of the sons of the members of each of the embassies so we were all swimming against our dads. We called our team the "internationals." As kids we had unlimited stamina and energy. We could swim faster than the old guys and since we swam together every day, we knew where each of us was at all times, like a well oiled machine. We were killers and never lost no matter who we swam against.

One of the dads was a customs official at the port of Rangoon. Whenever a ship would come into port, it was his job to inspect the cargo. He would then challenge the ships crew to a water polo match against our "international" team.

Memories of Burma

Of course they would always accept even if they didn't know how to swim. An invitation to spend a day at a private swim club after months at sea was too good to be true. Again, we never lost.

Upon entering the swim club one had to prove himself to be a member or a guest of a member. There was a sentry at the main entrance who would pass us into the club. On the next level down were male and female changing rooms. We would hang our suits on a clothes line and take a shower before suiting up and then down to the next level and the pool.

There is in Burma an insect known as a fire ant, a small red little fellow who travels in armies. Its bite is extremely painful. Somehow a large number of these ants found their way into my swim suit as it hung on the line and they began their attack about the time I arrived at pool side.

Gathered around the pool were a group of members, primarily English, many of whom regarded Americans as somewhat low class and quite uncouth. As the bites began I started to scream which got the attention of everyone at the pool. As my screaming intensified, I started beating on my crotch. I then jumped into the pool but that didn't stop the pain. I leaped back out of the pool and ran to the changing room screaming and beating my crotch all the way.

I finally rid myself of the insects but was sore for many days. Of course I was viewed as a typical American who embarrassed himself in the company of the club members. I don't think many people who were there even remembered the incident, but I surely do.

The Kokine Swimming Club

Memories of Burma

Machine Gun Bullets

I spent much of my time at the Flach residence. It was a mansion on some prime real estate located on a beautiful lake on the outskirts of Rangoon. The back yard of the home had a lower level to a tennis court and then another level down to the lake.

The family consisted of the parents, two sisters, Lauri and Edie who were about my age, fourteen to sixteen, and two brothers Butch and Spike, about seven and nine. Butch and Spike were total natives, more Burmese than Americans. They spoke fluent Burmese, dressed like local children and spent many hours at a nearby Buddhist temple.

Although they were younger, I enjoyed hanging around with them because they were somewhat as wild as I was. We did young boy pranks and were always looking for adventure. Maybe I also enjoyed being near their two sisters with whom I was infatuated.

One day we boys were swimming in the lake and discovered something buried in the mud in about three feet of water. It took Butch, Spike and me all of our efforts to pull the treasure from the lake. It was a small trunk and when we dragged it to shore and forced it open, we discovered military guns and ammunition. The trunk was most likely dumped by retreating Japanese soldiers near the end of WWII and had been in the lake for the past ten years.

Everything was rusted beyond recognition except the bullets that were wrapped in a protective covering and in excellent shape. What a great prize for young boys to discover. We were ecstatic as we divided the ammunition into three piles. I put mine into a small cloth bag and brought it to my house where I hid it from my parents.

I found out later that Mr. Flach found out about the bullets and made his boys use their slingshots to "shoot" them back into the lake, one at a time.

Many months later, after my family left Burma and were on our way back to the states, we had visited several countries. We finally landed at Orly airport in Paris in late May of 1958. Paris was under martial law as there was a major disturbance going on. Morocco was protesting the French presence in their country and there were police and army personnel on every street corner to keep the peace.

As we were about to clear customs, dad asked me if I had anything in my carry-on that would cause a problem because I had a habit of taking "souvenirs" from hotels we had stayed at in the countries we had visited.

I told my dad "no, I don't have anything—other than this bag of machine gun bullets." Dad hit the roof. I just brought out the worst in my normally easy going dad. He was cool though, as he put the bag into his pocket and calmly walked through customs. This was long before the airport security process that we now have to deal with.

Looking back, I can now imagine the penalty dad would have had to suffer for trying to smuggle machine gun bullets into a country that was under martial law. I'm sure it would have been severe.

The next day, dad made sure I was with him when we walked onto a bridge over the Seine River and dropped the precious bag into the water.

I wonder if someday, somehow, someone will find a bag of Japanese machine gun bullets in the river in Paris and think "what the hell?" Only a few of us will know the story. I love mysteries and this will be one of them.

The Flach's home at Inya Lake, Rangoon

Tennis Court Python

We were deep in the throes of the monsoon season. Rain storms almost every day, sometimes accompanied by strong winds. In late July we were near the last part of the rainy season, but still had about a dreary month of rain to go. Being in a jungle environment there was always tree and vegetation debris scattered everywhere after a storm. The rains would come and go—some days it would be sunny and other times it would rain for days.

One night there was a vicious storm followed by one of those warm sunny days that smelled so fresh and inviting that made one want to be outside doing something. We kids could get bored during the unrelenting storms, always looking for something active to do. We always had the Kokine swimming pool to fall back on but still needed diverse activities to keep our interest alive.

Bill Ramlow was a sixteen year old American whose father was an engineer living in Burma to help in the building of a dam to generate electricity for the country. The family lived in a quiet, remote area surrounded by a thick jungle and had a tennis court in their back yard.

Bill had asked my brother and me to "come over and play some tennis while we had a chance between storms."

Memories of Burma

When we got to Bill's house, we saw tree branches and other vegetation covering the court so we began to clear it away.

At the far end of the court lay a very large branch almost covering the entire width, perhaps ten feet or more.

As we went over to drag it from the area, it started to crawl away. Talk about being startled! At first we didn't recognize what was happening but suddenly we knew it was a snake. A very large snake.

What we had encountered was a Burmese Python, one of the world's largest snakes. It was not poisonous but being a python, it was still dangerous and scared the hell out of us.

It was obviously sunning and drying out from the previous rain storm and thankfully, not hungry as it slipped back into the jungle without attacking us.

Another encounter with the wildlife of Asia. Needless to say, we decided not to play tennis that day. As youngsters we were beginning to learn survival skills, becoming more aware of our environment and not taking anything for granted until we knew what was around us at all times. Of course, being young and immature, we forgot these lessons until the next time we were confronted by danger.

Clowning around at Chichi and Roberto's house

Back row from left: Chichi Arce, Jerry Olson, Bill Ramlow and Bruce Lindeman
Front row from left: David Olson (the author), Roberto Arce and Mike Weil

Halie Selassie

Early one morning at our house on Kokine Road our family woke up to quite a commotion coming from our front yard. Looking out the windows we could see soldiers with machine guns, poking through the hedges that lined the road. The servants' children were running about and chattering excitedly.

Our family had no idea why the soldiers were there or what they were doing. This was very unsettling because in Burma there were occasionally attacks by insurgents and bandits known as Dacoits, but those attacks usually took place in the north and not this close to Rangoon. There was also a concern of an invasion from neighboring China due to shared border disputes.

Standing on the veranda of the roof, we could see that other compounds on both sides of our house, as well as those across the road, were also occupied by armed soldiers who seemed to be hunkered down and just waiting. What they were waiting for, we did not know.

When the soldiers were confronted and asked what was going on, they ignored the questions and would not talk, probably because of their orders. Having the Burmese army in our front yard was both a relief and a concern. A relief as we felt we were protected if we needed to be and a concern because if there was some type of attack, we could be right in the middle of whatever was going to happen.

Eventually, a government motorcade drove down the road with flags flying and horns blaring. There were several sedans, American Cadillacs and Russian Zims being escorted by police motorcycles. Now, many people appeared along the roadway, waving Burmese flags and cheering as the motorcade passed.

Ronnie Carpenter, the son of our next door American neighbor, owned a Cushman Husky motor scooter. He and my brother Jerry jumped on the scooter and rushed behind the procession to see what was going on. Not having wheels, I was left behind.

I was told later that the motorcade ended about two miles north of our home at a religious site, a Buddhist temple called the "Peace Pagoda." The VIP was Haile Selassie, the emperor of Ethiopia who was being honored as a visiting chief of state.

Jerry and Ron got a chance to meet him. I was very envious for being left behind but the whole morning was very exciting none the less.

A party erupted in our compound and lasted throughout the day. It didn't take much to have a party in

Burma. The locals found any reason to be happy and to celebrate.

Since living in Burma, I've come to the realization that even though this is one of the poorest nations on the planet, the people are the happiest and nicest people you will ever encounter. They will use any situation to show that happiness and make others feel glad to just being there. All one has to do to get a smile from someone in Burma is to give one. It never fails!

Soldiers

The Fire Walking Ceremony

The major religion in Burma is Theravada Buddhism, but there are many minority groups that practice other religions. One of these is an Indian sect of Hinduism that observes the mysterious practice of fire walking.

This is done as a cleansing ceremony to purify the soul and to rid oneself of worldly sins. We were a part of a group of foreigners from the international community who attended an annual event being held at a meadow on the outskirts of Rangoon. Quite a few of us and the families from various embassies, as well as many local sightseers, attended.

A carnival atmosphere developed at the park where the ceremony was to take place. Amusement rides for the children such as a merry-go-round and a makeshift Ferris Wheel were erected. There were merchants selling treats such as candy, shaved ice and other tasty food items.

We were directed to a roped off area where we squatted on the ground around an area where a long pit was dug and then filled with hot coals. The pit was about fifteen feet long and five feet wide with a pit of water at one end for the disciples to step into as they finished their tortuous walk.

Men with rakes were grooming the hot coals and as

we sat about ten feet from it we could feel a burning sensation on our faces and any exposed skin as the heat flared up when they raked the coals. Almost unbearable!

In a nearby area, participants were undergoing additional acts of pain by having metal spears driven through their cheeks, lips and tongues and various other body parts.

One particular man had what was called "a thousand spears" puncturing his upper torso and held in place with a device that looked like two bicycle wheels that he supported with his hands and arms.

My friends and I watched as the spears were inserted into his torso and back. I had heard about this practice before-hand and always thought it was a trick of some kind but this was real.

Looking at the expression on the man's face it was obvious that he was in some sort of trance or perhaps he was heavily drugged. His eyes were partially rolled back and he showed no sign of being in any pain.

His ordeal began at mid morning and would last throughout the day as he walked around carrying his burden.

Only adult men, or disciples, as they were described to us, were actually allowed to walk on the coals. With each step they took we could see flames shoot up from their foot prints as they walked across the coals. Some ran through the pit but it was considered to be more holy to walk slowly.

Some firewalkers carried male children on their backs but children were not allowed to walk. Women were also not allowed to walk the coals but danced, gyrating alongside as if in a religious trance.

To us foreigners observing the entire ceremony was unbelievable and absolutely unforgettable. We were amazed that the firewalkers crossed the pit unscathed.

Hunting with Al Capone

Maurice Oakshot was an Englishman whose family had lived in Burma for many years, perhaps most of his life relative to his age of twenty one. He was one of the older members of the young people in our international community. It was not unusual for those of his age to socialize with the group since there were so few of us.

Several of us thought highly of Maurice as he knew Burmese culture and the language intimately. He was also a practicing veterinarian and had several clients among the foreign community, administering to their pets. He seemed awfully young to be allowed to practice medicine but we didn't know what the Burmese regulations were.

Maurice was quite overweight and had what looked like the bulbous nose of a heavy drinker although none of us ever saw him take a drink. His appearance reminded us of the American gangster Al Capone and thus—his nickname was born.

He was always referred to by his nickname and often someone in the group would say "What is his real name again?" Being called Al Capone never seemed to bother him and I think he rather enjoyed the endearment of having a celebrity's name.

Memories of Burma

It was 1956 and against Burmese law to possess a gun of any kind. Only police and army personnel could be armed. No private ownership was allowed. Somehow, Al came up with three rifles, probably from his veterinarian connections with the Burmese army, and he planned a hunting trip for myself and another American who lived in our compound, Ronnie Carpenter.

Ronnie had the attitude of a rebel, trying to pretend he was a tough guy. He was very handsome and exhibited the appearance of, if someone who observed him in the 1970's would call him a James Dean wannabe or perhaps, a Marlon Brando character. He sometimes had a pack of cigarettes rolled up in the sleeve of his tee shirt. He was usually lots of fun to be with.

I guess that I would describe myself as somewhat naïve. I just tried to get along with everyone being one of the youngest of the group at fourteen. I was kind of a tag along when I was with the older kids.

In order to get where we were going to hunt, we had to get on a bus which caused quite a commotion since we were three white guys with guns. I'm sure there was an uneasy feeling amongst the other riders until we finally got off the bus. We were now deep in a wild jungle several miles from Rangoon. This was an area of the country where few people would venture. We trusted that Al knew we were in no danger of attacks from bandits or insurgents.

The hunt was a bust. The only wildlife we saw all day were some large black birds, either crows or ravens that kept a safe distance from us.

As we were going back to the road to catch the bus to Rangoon, there were gunshots nearby—very close. We could hear the bullets hitting the trees near us. **WE WERE BEING SHOT AT!**

My first thought as I dropped facedown to the jungle floor was that this was an attack by the infamous insurgents we continually heard about.

Soon, we realized that there was only one gun being fired and it wasn't being directed at us. Carefully we crept to the road and saw a car parked there. Crossing the road, we could see a man with his back towards us. He still hadn't seen us and was firing a hand gun into the jungle.

Sensing that he wasn't alone, he turned to see three Caucasians with dirt on our clothing and faces, holding rifles and staring at him. Visibly shaken, he got into his car and slowly drove away.

"He looked like he was scared out of his mind," breathed Al. To tell the truth, we were all scared pretty badly after believing we had been shot at. Al surmised that he was doing the same thing we were. Sneaking out to a remote place to shoot his illegal weapon.

The three of us breathed a sigh of relief when the bus finally brought us back home.

The Si-Ca Man (The Side Car Man)

When we moved from our home on Kokine Road in 1957, it was somewhat traumatic for my brother Jerry, my sister Ginny and me. We were going to miss the third story roof veranda and the tree out front filled with the fruit bats.

We had grown to love hanging around the servants' quarters where we played poker for money with them. Somehow we never won. Ginny, who spoke better Burmese than Jerry and I, later told us that as we played, the servants' wives would stand behind us and tell their husbands what cards we held. All this in a Burmese dialect that Jerry and I didn't understand. We never caught on because they would let us win once in a while when the stakes were low. We were sad to leave the old home.

Dad worked at the Rangoon Technical High School as an advisor to the Director of Education of Burma, located about five miles away. Our new home was a just completed apartment complex next to the school, walking distance for dad each morning.

This left the car and our driver Maung Gyi, for mom and us kids to use as we needed. We kids didn't get permission to use the car during the day so we found our travel was accomplished by using the local bus, or by the old fashioned way, walking.

Riding a bus in Burma is an experience. They were always overcrowded with people hanging out of the doors and sometimes from the roof. The bus never really stopped at bus stops, just sort of slowed down and people would grab hold of a vertical bar near the door and swing on. The only exception would be if a child, a monk or an older person was waiting to board or depart.

Using British terminology, an apartment was called a flat. The floors were called levels and an elevator was called a lift. We were in the Okalapa flats, on the forth level. A stairway was available but we usually rode the lift.

Living there was not as comfortable as the house on Kokine Road. It was too clinical, very much like an American hotel. Our servants didn't like it either since they had been uprooted to move to a bungalow that was less like a home.

Since the building was a high rise of about fifteen levels, we had only one durwan or night watchman on duty. His job was to stay awake all night long to make sure that no one who didn't belong would climb the stairs or use the lift.

In order to make sure the residents knew that he was on the job and awake all night protecting them, he would ring a gong each hour, every hour all night long. Of course, he could have had an alarm clock to wake him up in time to ring his gong. It was hard to get used to waking up every hour to the sound of the gong, but what made it worse was what followed.

In Rangoon, there were a bunch of homeless dogs called Pye dogs. They were skinny, starving scavengers that ran in packs looking for food. They ran wild and were very troublesome but not dangerous. Each night when the durwan rang his gong, the Pye dogs would go into a frenzied howling and barking that lasted a long time. Then they went quiet until the next hour and the next gong would get them started again.

My dad's immediate boss, an American named Mr. Lubin who lived on the next flat above us, finally couldn't stand it any longer. He went crazy one night. We heard him yell, slam his door and take the lift to the parking area. He started his car and peeled out. Mr. Lubin wasn't the most personable character to begin with and that night he showed his true colors.

Acting like a madman, he wildly drove his car up and down the streets where the dogs were, trying to run them down. He only succeeded in creating more noise and howling. Ginny and I were at the window watching and rooting for the dogs the whole time.

Thus began our life at Okalapa flats.

Our brother Jerry had returned to the U.S. for his senior year of high school rather than continue the home schooling that we were receiving in Burma. So, I lost my best friend and protector for my final stay in Burma.

Our flat was not far from the Kokine Swimming Club where we kids spent much of our daytime hours. To get home from the club, we would ride a bus to the nearest stop and then walk about a half mile along a dense jungle path to the flat.

Often, it was dark when I began the walk. About half way along the path was a house at the top of a hill. I could usually see a lighted window through the trees. Each time I passed, a man's voice would start to moan and cry, sometimes he would scream. I called him Boog Yoke man. In my broken Burmese that meant crazy person. I found out later that the proper term for crazy is Yu Deh. He scared the wits out of me every time I passed his home. It reminded me of Halloween pranks used to scare young kids but this was real. Every time I passed his house, I was terrified. I began to think he was waiting for me to begin his moaning.

Memories of Burma

At the bus stop, before beginning the trek home, were a group of what were called Si-Ca drivers. That's a Burmese corruption of the word "side car" drivers. They were the taxi cab drivers who rode three wheeled bicycles waiting for fares. There was a seat at the back and facing the rear of the bike big enough for two.

Si-Ca drivers were also known as the criminal element of Rangoon. Anything anyone who would want to get anything in Burma through the black market had to contact these guys. Money laundering, after hour's petrol, anything.

These guys were athletic specimens, from riding bicycles all day. They were not burly like body builders but slender and very strong. You did not want to mess with them under any conditions.

One night I got off the bus and was about to walk down the path toward Boog Yoke, when one of the drivers yelled at me,"hey Myo Pu."

Now, this is not a nice thing to call a white guy. The driver obviously didn't know that I spoke some street Burmese, things I had picked up from my association with local kids that I played football (soccer) with. Myo Pu meant "white monkey." Kind of like calling a black person the "n" word.

Memories of Burma

I stopped, looked at him and yelled back "Kum ya apo chi gone chi que dee." This is a curse that loosely translates "I hope the crows shit on your head you male dog."

Total silence.

I had just cursed at the worst of the tough guys. I obviously wasn't a physical threat to anyone. A ninety-eight pound fifteen year old, and badly outnumbered. Probably not playing with a full deck either.

The silence didn't last long and he began to smile. He decided that if I had the guts to curse at him in his own language, well then, I was alright. We became fast friends and thereafter, every time I came to that bus stop and he was there, he would yell "hey Myo pu, laba laba."

"Hey white monkey, come here."

If he wasn't working a fare, he would give me a free ride home—right past Boog Yoke. No more fear as long as I had Si-Ca man as a friend.

A jungle path on the way home from the bus stop where I met the Si-Ca man.

Basketball with Red China

Chichi and Roberto Arce lived about one mile from our home at Okalapa flats. To get there we had to walk up a narrow and very dense jungle path. With the exception of a very few main streets in downtown Rangoon, there were no street lights to light the way. At night the path was pitch dark and was so overgrown with trees and vegetation that even during the day, the way was dimly lit.

I actually loved walking the path because I found it to be so mysterious yet comforting. The walk to the Arce's home was always very pleasant with one exception.

About half way between our homes was a school. We knew it as the "Chinese communist high school." Every time we passed the school, it seemed as though there were a group of kids playing basketball.

Chinese people are usually described as small in stature. Not true. These guys were tall, much taller than me anyway.

Each time we Americans would walk by on our way to and from the Arce's, the students would stop playing and stare at us with unfriendly looks on their faces and I suppose we replied in kind. I was never worried for my safety but was uncomfortable with the unspoken feelings that passed between us.

This was so silly. Just because they were from a communist country, they were still just kids, just like us. I'm sure that they heard the vicious, untrue stories about Americans as we heard about Chinese communists.

Anyway, this animosity continued for several months until one day when I was on my way to the Arce's, traveling alone along the dark jungle path. Suddenly, from around a bend, I encountered four of these students walking side by side, completely covering the path.

The looks on their faces suggested that I might be in trouble. I did the only thing I always did when meeting someone new. I smiled!

It worked every time. They smiled back and the next thing I knew, I'd been invited to play basketball and drink lemonade at their school. I was there for about an hour before continuing on to the Arce's.

Never under estimate the power of a smile.

The Chinese Graveyard

Hans Erickson and his sister Ula were two very close friends of ours. They were from Sweden and were already in Burma when we arrived in 1956. At sixteen Hans was two years older than I and Ula was a year older than her brother.

At the expense of using a stereotype I will describe Hans as a typical Swede. He was over six feet tall, blond, blue eyed and physically very fit. Ula was his mirror image. Both were extremely nice. They seemed always happy and pleasant. They both gave a long thought to what they were going to say when asked a question, thus giving the impression of being mentally slow. This was probably due to processing the English into Swedish but that was part of their allure. Everyone enjoyed being with them.

As juveniles at our swim club we each had to prove our swimming skills in order to earn our "Dolphin Badge" before being allowed to swim unchaperoned. The test included several things we had to do.

First, we had to swim the length of the pool, once on top of the water and once under water, about a forty foot distance. The next test was to jump into the pool with our clothes on over our swim suits, tread water and strip down to our suits. The final test was save someone who was in trouble while swimming.

The plan was to get behind the swimmer and secure them with an arm under the chin. Once this was done, the swimmer was supposed to submit and be brought to the side of the pool and to safety.

I was assigned to "save" Hans who was twice my size. I can still see him at the deep end of the pool, slapping the water with his hands, a big mischievous grin on his face as he called "come on Froggy, try to save me."

I had received the nickname of Froggy from my Yugoslavia friend Vlado. The first time he and I met was at the pool. I was wearing swim fins on my feet. After that, I was Froggy, but only to Vlado and Hans, and only at the pool.

Hans resisted all my attempts to bring him to the side of the pool and to "safety." Every time I got close to him, he would laugh and dunk me under the water. Finally, the life guard giving the test had to find someone to replace him in order for me to pass the test. I received my "Dolphin Badge" and Hans and I still remained best friends.

The Ericksons lived on a street that was only one block long. At the end of the street was a Chinese graveyard. The Ericksons had a difficult time hiring servants to work for them because of the graveyard. It was reported to be haunted and inhabited by spirits. Of course we kids thought it was really neat living next to a haunted graveyard and we weren't afraid of ghosts or "Nats" as they were called by the locals. I had already had an experience with a Nat on Kokine Road and never felt threatened.

Mr. Erickson would visit a men's billiard club one evening each week where he would meet other men, play billiards and have drinks. His club also showed movies for the children. It was really important for us kids to get a chance to see a movie, especially one from the States.

I always felt privileged to be invited to the Ericksons for dinner and afterwards to go to the movies with Hans. One evening, after dinner, Hans and I were waiting impatiently out by the car for his dad to take us to his club.

It was dusk and another beautiful Rangoon evening. I recall that the area around this neighborhood was usually hazy, with a mysterious reddish tint to the atmosphere, giving it a Brigadoon effect.

From where we were leaning against the car, we were looking at the house about thirty feet away. Suddenly, I noticed a woman carrying a baby and walking alongside the house. This was very strange because I didn't see her enter the compound which had a locked gate that protected the area from intruders.

She had just suddenly materialized with the house in her background. Then I thought that my eyes had deceived me because I could see lines and boards of the house right through her as if she was, not quite invisible, but transparent. She was walking away from where we stood so that her side and her back were toward us. As she reached the end of the house where she no longer had the house as a background, she vanished.

I was still staring at the missing space where she had been. My mouth wide open and my eyes as big as saucers. Finally I found my voice and whispered to Hans "Did you see that?"

Hans's reply was "no." It wasn't until later that his response bothered me. If he hadn't seen the figure he would have said something like, "what?" or "did I see what?" To say "no" meant he must have seen something but didn't want to believe it. He didn't want to discuss it with me either.

I have no memory of the rest of the evening—of what movie we saw or anything about that night other than the apparition at Hans' house. The only explanation I have is that in Burma, the sighting of supernatural or spiritual events is not only commonplace but acceptable. Perhaps the widespread belief in spirits allows these things to happen.

My reporting this as an actual happening and not a hallucination is not going to be accepted by most people, particularly those who have not lived in Asia. Many of us who have are more open minded because we have experienced similar events or have listened to testimonials from reliable persons who have.

Memories of Burma

Mr. Kronberg

My brother Jerry, our friend Bill and I used to go to a Chinese restaurant located on University Avenue across the street from Inya Lake, just on the outskirts of Rangoon. It was 1956. We used to play poker with the owner of the restaurant and one of us would be chosen to play. If he would win the game, we would get our meal for free. If he lost, we would pay double. I think that we probably broke even in the long run.

One evening after leaving the restaurant and walking down University Avenue towards a friend's house, we saw two European men pushing an old Volkswagen Bug. They were trying to get it started. One of them looked to be in his late twenties, the other a bit older. We helped to get the car started and they went on their way.

We found out later that the young man was Jan Kronberg. He was a representative of SAS Airlines from Copenhagen, Denmark. He was a close friend of the Lindemans who were also friends of our family.

Several months later we found out that Kronberg had been arrested and was in the Rangoon city jail. His crime was as follows.

The Burmese monetary system was in a shambles. Burmese money was of no value outside of Burma. What Kronberg had done was to sell an airline ticket to a client from Rangoon to London, stopping once in New Delhi. The transaction was done using Burmese Kyats.

Once the passenger arrived in India, they turned the remaining ticket in for a refund and then purchased a return ticket back to Rangoon. The refund was in Rupees which had a high value unlike Burmese Kyats.

I guess that is what is called laundering money and the Burmese government didn't like this at all because it further damaged the value of their currency. As a result, Kronberg languished in a Burmese jail for his part in the scam.

Easter was coming. Betsy Lindeman had organized our group of kids to visit Kronberg at the jail to cheer him up. He had been incarcerated for about six months and hadn't had many visitors.

There were about twenty of us and we were escorted to a quonset hut in a central area of the prison. We arrived on Good Friday and were allowed to celebrate High Mass inside the metal hut.

A priest was there to administer the service but the room was airless, without windows and too small for everyone to have a place to sit down. It was also very hot that day because the dry season was still with us, the monsoons hadn't yet begun. It was probably one hundred degrees inside. I was standing up at the back because of lack of seats and the heat finally got to me and I passed out.

When I came to, I was totally confused as to where I was. Lying on a cot, I sensed that I was all alone. I looked around and could see the bars of a jail cell. I got up and grabbed the door and it swung open. It wasn't locked.

This was like a dream, or rather a nightmare. I still hadn't put the situation into perspective. Since the door was open, I stuck my head out and looked down a long hall. What I saw stopped my heart stone cold.

I saw a long dark passageway and at the end, an open door with a view outside of a gallows with a hangman's noose, all silhouetted in the bright sunlight. Now I was not only confused but downright speechless. I closed the cell door and sat down on the cot to try to figure this out as Kronberg appeared outside the cell.

Noticing that the door was closed, he pulled a key from his pocket and unlocked the door. He brought me a bottle of goat's milk to revive me and then explained what had occurred.

He told me that when I fell unconscious, he had carried me to his cell and then went to purchase the milk. It seems that Kronberg, through his political connections and his ability to pay for services, had a key to every lock in the jail except the one to the outside. He had the run of the entire prison.

My breathing had now started to return to normal. I finally realized that no—I wasn't arrested and incarcerated in prison and no—that the gallows at the end of the hallway wasn't waiting for me. I suddenly felt a little bit better.

Kronberg was eventually released from jail and with a lot of help from the Lindeman family, returned to Denmark.

This had a big impact on my life as I decided to never do anything that would land me in prison. I also have totally lost any desire or taste for goat's milk.

Betsy's Story

Author's note: Following is information from Betsy Lindeman-Flint in 2010, regarding Mr. Kronberg's legal issues that I was unaware of during my teen years in Burma.

Jan Kronberg was arrested and languishing in jail awaiting trial. He was actually in jail for 18 months waiting for this trial. Eventually he was tried and fined the equivalent of $500 and deported. The night he was released he came to dinner at our house fully expecting to leave the country the next day. Mom and dad would take him to the airport. When he arrived at the airport he was unable to leave the country because he did not have a valid "exit" visa. I guess being deported didn't count. He went back to our house to get it straightened out. After six months or so of "you can't get an exit permit because you are in the country illegally" (having been deported) and explaining that he was willing to leave but needed the exit permit to do so, blah blah blah, he finally returned to Denmark.

Interestingly enough what he did is called tampering with the foreign exchange and many of the airlines were doing the same thing. The reason that the Indians and

Chinese were doing this was to get their money out of the country because there were constant (and historically true) rumors of a military takeover. When the coup actually happened most foreigners were given very little time (in some cases only a few hours) to leave the country taking nothing with them.

Our family visited Jan in prison often and brought him food, cough syrup (booze) and vodka-laden fruit each weekend that we were allowed to visit. It truly was a scary place to visit and one that I certainly would not be willing to call home.

Jan had two servants in jail; one to clean his cell (a convicted murderer) and a cook (I believe he was a rapist). His cell was on "death row" because these larger cells were more fitting for the token foreigner.

Betsy

Now this makes more sense to me (David) as to why I saw the gallows at the end of the hallway when I woke up after having passed out. The cell I was in was on death row.

Driving Cars

At fifteen years old I desperately desired to drive my dad's car. Like most kids at that age, I had decided that I already knew everything that was important in life including how to drive a car.

I tried several times to talk dad's driver, Maung Gyi, into letting me drive dad's car without success. One day he relented and finally agreed to let me back it out of the car park.

Disaster!

I wasn't as good a driver as I thought because I only moved the car about six feet before I turned the wheel too soon and crunched the fender against a pillar. The look on the face of Maung Gyi was like a photograph of devastation. I'm sure he was thinking "oh no, I just lost my job."

We briefly looked at each other and I must have shown fear because I had to face my dad. I also felt that I had done severe harm to Maung Gyi's position as driver because we all loved him as if he were family.

All of the local children began yelling noisily and the story of what had happened spread throughout the entire building in just a few minutes. I began to run up the stairs to be the first to tell my dad my side of the story. We met at the first level. He had already heard about it and as he looked at me I can still see the anger on his face as he reached for my throat.

He never touched me; he just paused, and proceeded down to the car park to see the damage to the car. The result was a severe tongue lashing for me and for Maung Gyi who was instructed never to allow me to drive the car again—ever.

I never begged Maung Gyi for that privilege again, knowing what the answer would be. Maung Gyi remained as our driver throughout our stay in Burma and was eventually promoted to an automobile repair instructor at dad's school after we left Burma in 1958.

Meanwhile, the good relationship I had enjoyed with the Erickson family was soon damaged due to irresponsible and downright juvenile teenage misjudgment.

As with most teenagers, we were always anxious to drive cars. I still hadn't learned my lesson. I was underage and had no license and obviously, no common sense. I had also lost any chance to drive dad's car.

Mr. Erickson owned two cars. One was a German Borgward, and the other a British Landrover. His son Hans did not have driving privileges either but that did not stop us.

Memories of Burma

Johnnie Seymore was the son of an American U.N. official who lived close to our home at the Okalapa flats. He would occasionally spend the night at our place. The two of us would wait until everyone was asleep and then sneak out sometime after midnight and walk the two miles to the Erickson home.

Hans would be waiting for us with the keys to the Landrover which we would quietly push out of the compound and down the road to a safe distance from the house. Hans would then start the car and we would proceed to drive around Rangoon for a few hours. Hans always drove as he wisely didn't trust us.

There were never any other cars on the roads at that time of the night—not even police cars. We had heard rumors that the police would lock the doors to the police station at sundown because it wasn't safe to be out after dark.

The three of us had several nights of blissful freedom as we drove around town, pretending to be adults and enjoying ourselves.

Until one night.

We were driving by the main Pagoda known as the Shwedagon at about 1AM, when we passed a car coming the other way. Hans cursed and suddenly pulled over to the side of the road and stopped the car.

Memories of Burma

"Hans, what are you doing?"

"It's my parents," he said.

They had heard us push the car from the house and tried to follow in the Borgward. They had been trying to find us for an hour.

Mrs. Erickson was livid and accused us as Americans of causing her son to do things that he would never do without our influence. I realized that she was probably right as Hans was easily lead, but he was two years older than Johnnie and me and should at least share the guilt.

She made us get out of the Landrover and walk home. Since there was considerable danger of being on the streets after dark, especially in the wee hours of the morning, this was not a good situation. A poor decision on the part of the Ericksons. I guess it was meant to be a punishment for what we had done.

I was never again invited to their home for dinner and a movie at the billiard club.

I also never tried to drive a car again for the rest of the time I lived in Burma as it got me into too much trouble.

Memories of Burma

Tattoos

When we first arrived in Rangoon and walked on the downtown streets, one thing we noticed immediately was what looked like blood stains on the sidewalk and on the streets. What had happened? There must have been people being murdered everywhere. All the locals seemed not to be affected by whatever carnage had occurred. In fact, no one seemed to notice. This was baffling to us as newcomers.

What we were seeing were stains from what was known as a local drug called betel nut. This was a mild narcotic, a berry that had a numbing effect when chewed and caused red saliva. The user would then spit, which would leave the bright red stain. Betel nut also caused the user's mouth and teeth to become very decayed so it was not difficult to recognize a chewer. It was not illegal to use and many of the locals did it.

Of all the wild things I participated in, I never tried betel nut. It was too gross to imagine. On my last trip to Burma in 2005, I noticed that the streets no longer had those red stains. Therefore, either the practice had been eliminated or has been declared illegal.

In those early days other things could be seen in the streets of Rangoon. Food sellers were everywhere, on every street. Everything from fruit sellers to local cigarettes and small cigars called cheroots and drinks made from squeezed sugar cane. I actually tried the sugar cane drink and it was very good. We had to be very careful of what we ate and drank from the streets because unsanitary preparations could cause dysentery.

As kids, we tried everything to eat that we could from the streets, and yes, we suffered mild cases of "the trots," but I think we developed immunity to the affliction because of our youth and being exposed so often as we tried new foods. We were becoming natives. It wasn't too long before I ate and drank from the street vendors with no ill effects at all.

Another activity on the streets was the barbers, who would cut hair, trim beards and shave faces. My dad, who was an amateur photographer, took several pictures of them and titled them "Burma Shave." He submitted one photo to a national magazine, but nothing ever came of it. I thought it was clever though.

One day our American friend Bill Ramlow and I were walking down one of these Rangoon streets and came across a man doing tattoos. Tattoos were considered to be a spiritual protection from evil spirits and bad diseases and were popular with young men.

Memories of Burma

Bill and I decided to get a tattoo of our names on our arm. Now this was 1956 and the fear of HIV and AIDS was unknown. The street artist had only one needle that he used for all of his clients, probably without cleaning before each use. Being young and naïve, we never questioned this.

We had to write our names on a piece of paper so he could duplicate the English words. Bill went first and had his name successfully written on his arm.

When it was my turn, the tattoo artist got as far as writing DA before I was violently grabbed from the stool I was on and shaken by an unknown person. It turned out he was an American agent for Pan Am Airlines named Al Lorenzo, working through the American embassy. He began yelling at us about how we were ruining our lives and shoved Bill and me into his car. He had been passing by when he saw the stupid thing we were doing and decided to interfere. He drove us home and I never saw him again.

Meanwhile, I now had a tattoo of "DA" on my arm. I covered it with a bandaid hoping my parents wouldn't see it. Eventually I would have to own up to it and wasn't sure how that would work out.

My friends at the swimming pool noticed the DA and thought it was great because the Burmese word DAH was pronounced the same way and it meant a big knife or a sword. So for a while I was known as "the DAH."

Finally I realized that it wasn't going to go away so one day I went downtown, found another tattoo artist and had him complete the word to DAVE. My parents didn't like me having a tattoo but what was done was done. Oh well!

When our reunion group gets together at one of our gatherings, someone usually says "hey Dave, hey Bill, let's see your tattoos." We all laugh at the story.

Burma Shave

Home Schooling

Going to school in Burma was a new experience. I was being home schooled by my mother, along with my brother Jerry and our friend Bill Ramlow. We were taking correspondence courses from the University of Nebraska for our tenth/eleventh grade high school classes. It was a slow process because it took a long time for our courses to arrive from the States due to the slow mail system as well as mailing back the tests to be scored and recorded.

We also found the classes to be very boring because the lessons were so easy. I got to the point of purposely answering some of the test questions wrong just so I wouldn't have a perfect score. An example of this was the question "what is the main source of energy for our solar system?" The correct answer should have been "the Sun." I submitted my answer as "wheaties." The response from the U. of Neb. was not very friendly and my mom wasn't too happy either.

After my brother Jerry left Burma to return to the states for his senior year of high school, our dad and mom decided that I should go to an organized school to complete my tenth grade education. They arranged for me to attend the Methodist English High School located in downtown Rangoon.

This was a British public school and the curriculum was totally strange to me. The measurements and the math were all done using the metric system which I didn't understand. As the students walked the halls between classes, we were kept under the watchful eye of a prefect, also known in the states as a hall monitor. These guys were vicious and unrelenting. If we were caught talking in the hallway, we were put on report and would be disciplined.

I was not used to these strict rules and had some problems. In the classroom we had to stay silent until the teacher arrived. We then would applaud until she/he was seated. In Minnesota on the first day of school we would fill out a form that declared our nationality. A similar form was filled out here and I declared myself to be "Norwegian."

The teacher said "we have a young Norwegian lad in class today. What part of Norway are you from?" "Oh" I said, "I've never been to Norway."

She took offense and thought I was being smart with her and was trying to make a fool of her in front of the class. So on my first day of school, I got off on the wrong foot and never recovered. Within a fortnight I was declared "unfit" and was no longer a student there.

Memories of Burma

Next, dad and mom sent me to the Kirkham private school which tutored foreign students. This was where I had wanted to go in the first place because all of my international friends went there, especially the Flach sisters with whom I was totally in love.

That didn't work out either because the Kirkham's didn't have the curriculum from the University of Nebraska that I was enrolled in, so I was back at home being schooled by my mother.

Actually this worked out best for me because as I mentioned, the courses were easy and I was done with my lessons in two hours and then was free to go the swim club and wait for the Kirkham school kids to show up two hours later.

Life was good!

Alan Cho

One of our Burmese friends was named Aung Aung Cho, known to us as Alan Cho. Alan was about 18 years old. He was a great tennis player and was the champion of Burma. He was the best player in the country.

His family was very wealthy. They lived in a beautiful home and had a tennis court in their front yard. Alan would invite several of us to play tennis at his house. Bill Ramlow, Ronnie Carpenter, my brother Jerry and myself. The four of us were beginners and looking back, I realize now just how lousy we were as tennis players.

Alan must have enjoyed our company because as good as he was, he never criticized us but helped us to play better.

The weather in Rangoon was always hot, even during the monsoon season with humidity above 80%. During the dry season the temperature would reach 100 degrees. It was the only time we could count on being able to play tennis.

As we learned the game at Alan's house, their servants kept a steady stream of ice cold lemonade delivered to courtside to keep us refreshed.

Alan played in several tournaments and my memory tells me that he won them all. I recall the tournament he played for the championship of Burma which he won when his opponent withdrew in the final set because of severe cramps.

This would be akin to winning the U.S. Open in the States. All of Alan's friends were overjoyed. One of our group, Ray, owned a small British car called a Morris Minor. After the match, Ray offered to drive us to the bus stop, about one half mile away. There were not enough seats in the car for everyone so three of us climbed on the rear bumper for the short ride to the stop.

This became another one of my poor adolescent decisions. The trunk of the car, or rather the "boot" (as the English call it) is smooth with nothing to hold onto. The exuberance of Alan's win carried over to those of us celebrating. Ray began to drive wildly, making zigzagging turns and I fell off of the car at about 25 miles an hour, severely injuring my back.

I didn't want to tell my parents what had happened and suffered with the injury for several weeks. Eventually, not being able to conceal the pain, I confessed and was admitted to the Methodist English Hospital where I received radiation treatment three days a week for several months. Being a young boy of 15, I eventually healed, however now at 68 years old I feel back pains often that I attribute to that injury.

Alan eventually received a tennis scholarship to the university at Kalamazoo, Michigan. Once he left Burma we never heard from him again.

My last clear memory of him was when we invited him as a guest to watch a movie at the Kokine Swimming Club one evening. The movie was the Hollywood production of Show Boat. Alan became very agitated that night because of the racial undertones that the movie revealed. It still showed existing attitudes by the whites toward the blacks in the south in the early 1900's.

What we kids were unaware of was the Kokine Swimming Club, set up by the British, was a white only membership and restrictive towards people of colour. They not only were not eligible to be members but not allowed to swim as guests.

An example of British policies of racial discrimination that deeply affected relationships was an incident involving my brother Jerry. At sixteen years old Jerry had a girlfriend he liked very much. Her name was Marika Barrington. Her father was English and her mother, Burmese. Mr. Barrington was an official in the Burmese government and was a very influential and powerful person in the country.

Marika was one of the most beautiful girls we had ever seen. We all said that she looked like a young Elizabeth Taylor.

Jerry had invited Marika to swim at our club but at the main entrance, she was denied admittance. She was totally humiliated and Jerry was very embarrassed. Marika dissolved any relationship with all of our "international" community. We never saw her again.

We were all angered by this but still didn't realize that we were part of the problem. Even though we complained, we had allowed this to occur, yet still continued our membership in the swimming club.

The Kwongs

Each summer, beginning in June of 1956, our friend Jai Kwong would return home to Rangoon from school in England. We kids in the international community would all rejoice at his homecoming because he was one of our dearest friends.

Mr. Kwong was a successful businessman and quite wealthy. Jai and I were about the same age having both been born in 1941.

The Kwong family consisted of Jai, his younger sister Mei Mei, and younger brother Dee Dee. Their names had diminutive meanings in Chinese. Jai meant "first son," Mei Mei meant "little sister," and Dee Dee meant "little brother." Mei Mei was about ten years old and Dee Dee a year older.

My memory of the younger kids was that when we older kids would be enjoying the backyard swimming pool at their house, the little ones would be peeking through the shrubbery bordering the pool with big, inquisitive eyes watching. They were the cutest little kids I had ever seen.

I hadn't learned about the story of the Kwong's swimming pool until a 2007 reunion in Virginia, U.S.A. when Jai told us what had occurred.

Memories of Burma

The racial rules of the swim club that excluded non-whites from membership were unknown to us kids. A well kept secret never spoken about. Jai was extremely unhappy to find that his family was not allowed to join the club. When Jai confronted his dad, Mr. Kwong said "No problem, I'll build you your own pool." So when he was back from school, we swam exclusively at his house. Again, we kids were naive about the racial attitudes of the British colonial system and never questioned their policies. As I mentioned, we didn't learn this until 2007.

There were several large German shepherd guard dogs used to patrol the club's property. Sometimes they would be loose and charge us at pool side. They probably just wanted to play with us but we didn't take any chances and jumped into the pool. The dogs would bark at us until the servants came to capture them and put them on leashes.

Another childhood memory was eating lunches at the Kwong's home. The dining area was a large room with a huge circular table with a lazy Susan. Exotic dishes of Chinese food crowded the moveable table. The one dish I remember most was called "thousand year old egg." It wasn't really that old—maybe a month or so. I guess the egg would be buried in a special container and left for a period of time until it would ripen into an edible state. I never developed a taste for it although it was considered a delicacy.

Eating lunch at the Kwong's was always a special treat!

The Kwong's would occasionally have special guests at their home. Once, while swimming, we got a glimpse of someone we knew was famous but couldn't place her. After whispering with each other, we realized it was the American singer/actress Eartha Kitt. Another house guest whom I actually met was an American athlete who at that time was called "the fastest man alive" as he had just broken a world track record of some kind. His name was David Simms.

My remembrances of being a guest at the Kwong residence were among the fondest memories of those idyllic and halcyon days in Burma.

Leaving Burma

One day in April of 1958, dad came home with some very sad news. We were told that we had to leave Burma and that we had only two weeks to settle all of our affairs and be gone.

The news came from the Burmese government via the American Intelligence Agency. It seems that a military coup was about to occur, where the Burmese government was about to change hands.

Prime Minister U Nu was to be replaced by General Ne Win who would take over in a "caretaker government." We were told by our sponsor, the Ford Foundation, that for our own safety we were being recalled to the States.

Our family was actually fortunate to have two weeks to sell what we could and ship whatever was left back to the States. We were never in danger of any violence, at least to my knowledge, but having only two weeks to get our affairs in order was very stressful.

During that time, dad and mom acted very efficiently. For example, they hired a team of Burmese carpenters to seal up our household belongings such as furniture and appliances within a large shipping crate to be sent by ocean liner to our home in the States.

Dad had the foresight to have the crate made of teak wood for two good reasons. Teak is one of the most durable woods in the world. The shipping crate would therefore be safe from the elements during the ocean voyage. Teak wood is grown only in Southeast Asia and is quite valuable.

The second reason was that when the crate arrived in the States, we could disassemble it and use the teak wood for building furniture and other projects without having to pay import taxes on the expensive wood.

At the time, the only thing we kids were concerned with was that we had to leave our beloved Burma and all our friends that we had shared so many experiences with. All the other families had to leave as well with the realization that we would probably never see each other again. We were being scattered to all corners of the planet. North and South America, Europe and other countries in Asia.

I believe that the Kwong family had only six hours to leave. Mei Mei had been raised by her Burmese Amah and they were suddenly separated, never to see each other again. She told me in 2005 that it was a very traumatic experience for her.

Thinking back to the day we first arrived in Burma in 1956, I recall all the international children that came to the airport to welcome us, a totally unexpected pleasure. I also remember that throughout the next two years all the times that we children would descend upon the airport to welcome or say farewell to friends. The farewell times were usually sad and tearful.

On those visits, we kids were quite unruly and undisciplined because we would rush right through customs and out onto the airport tarmac to escort our friends to the airplane or to be waiting for them as they deplaned.

I can still recall hearing an angry voice on the loudspeaker urging "Will the American children please return to the terminal immediately." Somehow we never got into trouble over this. In today's world we would undoubtedly be arrested.

Because of the political situation, each departure was very emotional, as this one was. As I sat in the aircraft looking out the window at the sad faces and waving friends, I felt the tears come.

However, sometime after we were out of Burmese airspace and on our way to Calcutta and then onward to New Delhi, with the knowledge that my parents had planned a month long trip through Asia, the Mid-East and then Europe before heading home to the States, I began to look forward to the next adventure.

Memories of Burma

I could hardly wait for the fun to begin—again.

Burmese farmers and their water buffalo